DISAPPOINTING AFFIRMATIONS

A Hilariously Honest Journey

CLEVERLY
DISGUISED
= as a =
responsible
Adult

Introduction

Welcome to Disappointing Affirmations, where we dive headfirst into the delightful chaos of life, love, and everything in between! This isn't your average self-help book filled with glossy platitudes and feel-good mantras. Instead, it's a tongue-in-cheek collection of affirmations that celebrate the beautifully messy, often ridiculous, and sometimes disappointing aspects of our existence. In a world that often demands relentless positivity, it's refreshing (and oh-so-necessary) to acknowledge our not-so-perfect moments with humor and honesty. Here, we'll poke fun at the little mishaps, the awkward encounters, and the crushing disappointments that come with being human. From love that feels like a sitcom episode gone wrong to friendship dynamics that resemble a reality show, every page is a reminder that it's okay to laugh at our struggles and embrace the chaos.
These affirmations are not about dismissing the tough times; they're about recognizing that life can be a series of comic misadventures. They encourage us to find solace in our shared experiences and to celebrate our imperfections with a hearty chuckle. Whether you're navigating the ups and downs of romance, battling the unpredictability of work life, or simply trying to figure out how to make it through the day without tripping over your own feet, you'll find a kindred spirit in these pages.
So, grab a cup of your favorite beverage, get cozy, and prepare to embark on a journey that invites you to embrace the disappointment, laugh at the absurdity, and ultimately find joy in the chaos of life. Because sometimes, the best way to deal with the trials and tribulations is to acknowledge them, share a laugh, and remember that we're all in this together. Welcome to a world where humor meets honesty, and where disappointing affirmations become a source of unexpected strength!

PROCRASTINATION

"Today's plan: conquer the world!

Tomorrow's plan: start with the laundry."

"Why do today what can be put off until

tomorrow? It's all about priorities."

"Procrastination is just my way of managing

expectations—mostly my own."

"The early bird gets the worm, but the late bird

enjoys a lovely brunch."

"Why rush? Life's all about savoring that guilty

pleasure of doing nothing."

I'm Just
WTF-iNG
My Way
THROUGH LiFE

"Some say procrastination is a crime. I prefer to think of it as creative time management."

"It's not procrastination; it's a carefully curated experience of delayed gratification."

"Why stress today when you can worry about it tomorrow?"

"Procrastination: the art of keeping up with yesterday's goals."

"Chasing dreams is great, but have you ever tried napping instead?"

PROUD
Supporter
OF MESSY
Hair And
SWEATPANTS

SELF-DOUBT

"Confidence is overrated; the thrill of doubt is where the excitement lies."

"Self-doubt: the only thing that keeps me humble and mildly paralyzed."

"Trusting myself is a daily challenge, but hey, at least it keeps things interesting."

"Why stand tall when you can crouch in uncertainty?"

"Every moment of self-doubt is just a reminder that I'm human—what a relief!"

Hold On
LET ME
Overthink
THiS

"Life's tough, but so is living with the constant 'am I good enough' question."

"Doubt is just my brain's way of keeping me entertained with existential crises."

"Who needs confidence when self-doubt keeps things spicy?"

"Each moment of uncertainty is just a chance for growth… or a good nap."

"Self-doubt is my trusty sidekick, always reminding me of my limitations."

"Maybe I'm not meant to shine; maybe I'm just here for the ambiance."

I'm Just
WTF-iNG
My Way
THROUGH LiFE

FAILURE

"Why succeed when failing offers such delightful stories?"

"Every setback is just a setup for a better punchline later."

"Failure is proof that I'm trying… and trying really hard to mess it up."

"Success may be great, but failure has better tales to tell."

"If at first you don't succeed, redefine success and try again."

"Failure isn't the end; it's just the universe's way of saying, 'Not today.'"

BEING A Functional ADULT EVERY Day Seems A BIT EXCESSIVE

"Every failure is just a chance to improve my

'what-not-to-do' list."

"Success is temporary; failure is a lifelong

companion."

"At least failure knows how to show up

uninvited and steal the spotlight."

"Failure is just another way to say, 'Well,

that was unexpected!'"

"Turning failures into lessons is like turning

lemons into lemonade—with a twist of

regret."

"Success may be the goal, but failure has all

the best anecdotes."

BODY IMAGE

"Every body is a good body—especially if it enjoys pizza."

"Flaws are just personality traits on my skin; they deserve love too."

"Mirror, mirror on the wall, who needs perfection anyway?"

"Beauty is skin deep, but tacos are forever."

"A little extra fluff is just a sign of good taste—literally."

I'm fat
but identify as
Skinny
♥ I am ♥
TRANS-SLENDER

"Confidence is just knowing how to work it, even when you're feeling a little 'meh.'"

"Each wrinkle is a badge of wisdom—and maybe too many laughs."

"Beauty standards are just suggestions; I prefer to create my own."

"My body is a wonderland… mostly of snacks and comfy clothes."

"Loving my body means accepting that it loves carbs just as much as I do."

"Every curve has a story, and mine are all about late-night snacks."

Kinda Sweet Kinda Savage

RELATIONSHIPS

"Love is blind, but it's also really good at making questionable choices."

"Communication is key, but sometimes so is a good excuse for silence."

"Every fight is just a chance to practice my debate skills."

"Love is about compromise… and learning when to let the other person have the last fry."

"Relationships are like plants; sometimes they just need a little space… or a lot of water."

"Every argument is a chance to show off my impressive skill in stubbornness."

IT'S FINE

I'm fine

EVERYTHING'S

fine

"Compromise is just another word for 'I really don't want to watch that movie.'"

"Love means accepting each other's quirks—especially the ones that drive you crazy."

"Every relationship comes with baggage—just make sure it's not a suitcase full of drama."

"Sometimes love is just agreeing on where to eat… and calling it a win."

"The best relationships are built on laughter and the occasional eye roll."

"Love is like a dance—sometimes it's graceful, other times it's just a lot of stumbling."

PLEASE
don't talk
— TO ME —

WORKPLACE STRUGGLES

"Work is where dreams go to take a nap...

right at their desks."

"Every coworker has quirks; it's just part of

the charming workplace experience."

"Success at work is about pretending you

have it all figured out—until you don't."

"The best part of working from home?

Pajamas are always appropriate."

"Who needs motivation when there's a coffee

machine in the break room?"

"The office is a stage, and I'm just here for

the performance."

LET'S KEEP THE

Dumbfuckery

— TO A —

MINIMUM TODAY

"Today's goal: surviving the workday without caffeine-induced panic."

"Success is all about faking it until you make it… or until lunch."

"The office is a jungle, and I'm just trying to avoid being eaten alive."

"Every meeting is just a chance to practice nodding while thinking about snacks."

"Working hard or hardly working? At least I'm committed to one of them."

MENTAL HEALTH

Self-care is important; let's start with a nap

and call it a win."

"Mental health days are just a fancy way of

saying 'I'm tired of adulting.'"

"Some days are better than others; today is

just here to keep things interesting."

"It's okay to not be okay; it just makes for

more interesting stories."

"Some days require all the coffee, while

others just need comfy blankets."

Keep TALKING I'm DIAGNOSING You

"Self-compassion is about giving yourself a

break, preferably with cookies."

"It's perfectly fine to have days where the only

achievement is getting out of bed."

"Taking care of your mind is important;

snacks help, too."

"Mental health matters, even if it means

binge-watching your favorite show."

"It's okay to feel lost; it just means you're on

an unexpected adventure."

"The ups and downs of mental health are just

life's way of keeping it real."

Do not disturb.

My Peace • My Joy • My Vibe

AGING

"Aging gracefully? More like stumbling with style."

"With age comes wisdom, but also the knowledge that naps are essential."

"Every gray hair is just a reminder of the adventures had along the way."

"Aging is nature's way of saying, 'You've earned those laugh lines!'"

"Embracing age means celebrating every imperfect moment of this wild ride."

"Growing older is just leveling up in the game of life—bonus points for humor."

I'M REALLY NOT
FUNNY
I'M JUST MEAN
AND PEOPLE THINK
I am joking

"Every decade brings new experiences—

mostly involving sore joints."

"Aging is inevitable; gracefully is optional, and

fun is mandatory."

"Every birthday is just another excuse for

cake and more naps."

"Growing older means getting better at

ignoring what doesn't serve you."

"Life's a party, and aging is just the confetti—

messy but fabulous."

"With age comes the joy of knowing what

truly matters—like good snacks."

Kinda Classy Kinda hood :)

MOTIVATION

"Some days require extra motivation; other days just a coffee will do."

"Every little step counts, even if it's just from the couch to the fridge."

"Motivation is great, but let's not forget the power of procrastination."

"Sometimes the best motivation comes from the thought of dessert."

"Motivation is just another word for 'let's see how little we can do today.'"

"The secret to staying motivated? Bribery with snacks."

PROUD
Supporter
OF MESSY
Hair And
SWEATPANTS

"Every little effort is a step in the right direction—mostly towards the fridge."

"Sometimes the only motivation needed is the promise of a cozy blanket."

"Finding motivation can be a challenge; that's why coffee is essential."

"Motivation is about balance; let's not forget to prioritize relaxation."

"Motivation is just another fancy word for 'don't forget the snacks.'"

I was born
TO BE WILD
BUT ONLY UNTIL
9 pm or so

HEALTH AND FITNESS

"Every workout is just an opportunity to

question my life choices!"

"Why aim for fitness goals when I can

embrace my couch potato status?"

"At least I'm consistently inconsistent with my

exercise routine!"

"Fitness is just a series of awkward moves

and unexpected spills."

"Who needs a six-pack when I can have a

fun-loving muffin top?"

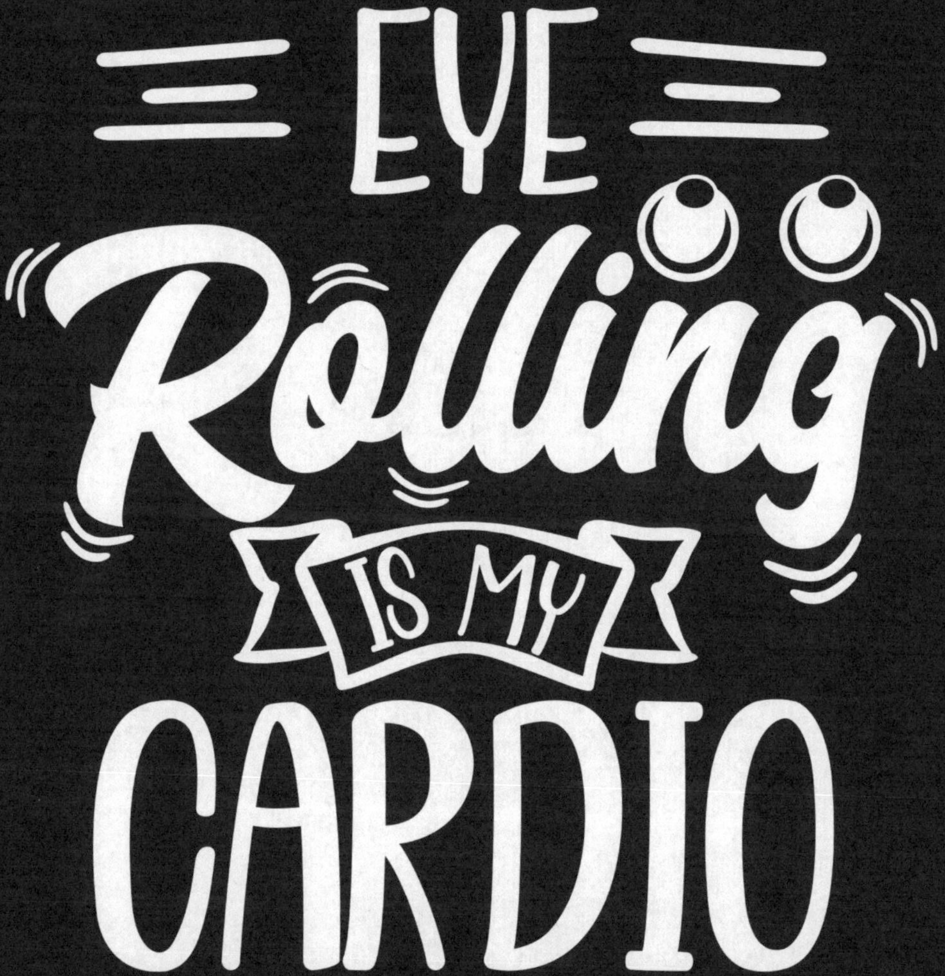
EYE
Rolling
IS MY
CARDIO

"Every failed diet is just a chance to savor life's little pleasures!"

"Health is a journey; I'm just enjoying the scenic route!"

"If sweating is the goal, I'm definitely winning —during my naps!"

"Every workout mishap is a reminder that laughter is the best cardio!"

"If self-care means bubble baths, I'm practically a wellness guru!"

SOCIETY AND EXPECTATIONS

"Society's standards are overrated; I'm just here for the laughs!"

"Why fit in when I can stand out as a beautifully flawed individual?"

"Every societal expectation I ignore is just another step towards freedom!"

"If everyone's doing it, I'll probably be going the opposite direction!"

"Who needs validation from others when I can embrace my own weirdness?"

I HATE

- morning people -

OR MORNINGS

or people

"At least I can say I'm consistently defying

expectations!"

"Society's norms are just guidelines; I prefer

to write my own rules!"

"Every time I rebel against expectations, I

create a great story!"

"Why conform when I can dance to the beat

of my own drum?"

"If society's rules are a game, I'm just here for

the bloopers!"

Don't
Study
me
you won't
Graduate

PARENTING

"Every parenting fail is just a sign of my commitment to chaos!"

"If I can't be the perfect parent, I'll at least be the fun one!"

"At least my kids will have hilarious stories to tell their therapists!"

"Who knew parenting could be this entertainingly unpredictable?"

"Every parenting mishap adds to my growing collection of funny moments!"

I looked up
MY SYMPTOMS
TURNS OUT
I Just
have kids

"If parenting is a circus, I'm just trying to juggle it all with flair!"

"At least I'm not alone in my journey of chaotic parenthood!"

"Every time I lose my patience, I'm just adding to the family lore!"

"If my kids are learning from my mistakes, they'll be set for life!"

"Parenting might not come with a manual, but at least it's full of laughs!"

Parenting style somewhere between NO! DON'T! and oh whatever

PERSONAL GROWTH

"Every setback is just a hilarious plot twist in my journey to growth!"

"If I can't get it right, at least I'll learn something funny!"

"Who needs self-improvement when I can just enjoy the chaos?"

"At least every mistake adds to my collection of life lessons!"

"If I can't achieve my goals, I'll just celebrate the journey!"

She believed
SHE COULD
BUT SHE COULDN'T
BE bothered
So She didn't

"Every time I stumble, I'm just adding to my character development!"

"Who knew that personal growth could come with so many laughs?"

"If I can't figure it out, I'll at least make it entertaining!"

"At least my growth journey is filled with colorful missteps!"

"If progress is slow, I'll just enjoy the scenery along the way!"

Just because
I AM AWAKE
DOESN'T MEAN
I want To do Things

TIME MANAGEMENT

"Every late arrival is just my personal brand of

dramatic flair!"

"If I can't manage my time, at least I can

manage my humor!"

"At least my chaotic schedule keeps life

unpredictable!"

"Who knew that time management could lead

to such amusing outcomes?"

"Every missed deadline is just another

chance to embrace spontaneity!"

Monday
SHOULD BE
Optional

"If I can't stick to a plan, I'll just enjoy the improvisation!"

"At least my disorganization provides comic relief for my friends!"

"Who needs a planner when I can live in delightful chaos?"

"Every time I'm late, I'm just adding to my collection of excuses!"

"If time isn't on my side, I'll just laugh my way through it!"

I AM A GREAT

MULTITASKER

I CAN LISTEN,

IGNORE

& FORGET

ALL AT THE SAME TIME

SOCIAL ANXIETY

"If I fumble my words, it's just my mind doing

a happy dance!"

"Every anxious moment is just my body

preparing for an impromptu performance!"

"If my palms sweat, it's just a sign of my

superhuman excitement!"

"Every awkward silence is just a chance for

inner comedy to shine!"

"If my heart races, it's just the thrill of living

out loud!"

FUN FACT:

I really don't care

"Every blush is just my body's way of

expressing its creativity!"

"If I feel out of place, at least my humor keeps

me grounded!"

"Every nervous laugh is just me embracing

the beautiful chaos!"

"If my mind wanders, it's just plotting my next

comedic masterpiece!"

"Every socially awkward moment is just a plot

twist in my comedy series!"

I'M NICER

than my

FACE

looks

DREAMS AND ASPIRATIONS

"If my dreams seem wild, at least they keep life interesting!"

"Every unfulfilled goal is just a chance for comedic plot twists!"

"If my ambitions waver, I'll just laugh and try something else!"

"Every failed attempt is just a funny story waiting to be told!"

"If my dreams shift, I'll just go with the flow like a leaf in the wind!"

I hope
KARMA
SLAPS YOU IN FACE
before I do

"Every aspiration is just a stepping stone to hilarious growth!"

"If I can't reach the stars, I'll settle for a delightful sky!"

"Every dream is just a journey filled with unexpected surprises!"

"If I can't find my path, I'll just enjoy wandering aimlessly!"

"Every aspiration is just a hilarious chapter in my life's book!"

Being an
adult is like
The dumbest
THING I'VE
EVER DONE

ROMANTIC REALITIES

"Love is like a rollercoaster, and I forgot to buckle my seatbelt!"

"Every relationship is just a game of who can ignore the red flags better!"

"Love at first sight? More like love at first awkward conversation!"

"If my heart gets broken, at least I'll have a great story to tell!"

"Every romantic comedy is just a beautiful lie wrapped in laughter!"

DON'T RUSH ME

I'M WAITING FOR THE

last minute

"Every love song reminds me that I'm still waiting for the punchline!"

"If my partner forgets anniversaries, I'll just celebrate the 'not-so-special' moments!"

"Every romantic gesture gone wrong is just a comedic skit waiting to happen!"

"If love feels like a rollercoaster, I'm holding on for dear life with a grin!"

"Every 'it's not you, it's me' conversation is just a chance to practice my poker face!"

SORRY FOR THE
mean,awful
(BUT WE'RE BEING HONEST)
Accurate
Thinks I said

Made in United States
Troutdale, OR
11/06/2024

24516900R00042